Animal Groups

A Pod of Dolphins

By Matthew Fenner

Please visit our website, www.garethstevens.com. For a free color catalog of all our high-quality books, call toll free 1-800-542-2595 or fax 1-877-542-2596.

Library of Congress Cataloging-in-Publication Data

Fenner, Matthew, 1970-
 A pod of dolphins / Matthew Fenner.
   p. cm. — (Animal groups)
 ISBN 978-1-4339-8215-6 (pbk.)
 ISBN 978-1-4339-8216-3 (6-pack)
 ISBN 978-1-4339-8214-9 (library binding)
 1. Dolphins—Juvenile literature. 2. Social behavior in animals—Juvenile literature. 3. Animal societies—Juvenile literature. I. Title.
 QL737.C432F46 2013
 599.53—dc23

2012022891

First Edition

Published in 2013 by
Gareth Stevens Publishing
111 East 14th Street, Suite 349
New York, NY 10003

Copyright © 2013 Gareth Stevens Publishing

Designer: Sarah Liddell
Editor: Greg Roza

Photo credits: Cover, p. 1 Willyam Bradberry/Shutterstock.com; p. 5 James Steidi/Shutterstock.com; p. 7 Mike Price/Shutterstock.com; p. 9 guentermanaus/Shutterstock.com; p. 11 Dennis van de Water/Shutterstock.com; p. 13 © iStockphoto.com/DavidMSchrader; p. 15 Croisy/Shutterstock.com; p. 17 (dolphin) Steve Noakes/Shutterstock.com; p. 17 (fish) DJ Mattaar/Shutterstock.com; p. 19 Elena Larina/Shutterstock.com; p. 20 Condor 36/Shutterstock.com; p. 21 Xavier MARCHANT/Shutterstock.com.

All rights reserved. No part of this book may be reproduced in any form without permission in writing from the publisher, except by a reviewer.

Printed in the United States of America

CPSIA compliance information: Batch #CW13GS: For further information contact Gareth Stevens, New York, New York at 1-800-542-2595.

Contents

Sea Mammals 4
Oceans and Rivers 8
Dolphin Friends 10
Superpods! 12
Dolphin Sounds 14
Body Language 18
Meet the Killer Whale! 20
Glossary 22
For More Information 23
Index 24

Boldface words appear in the glossary.

Sea Mammals

Dolphins aren't fish. They're sea **mammals**. Dolphins are some of the smartest and friendliest wild animals on Earth. They travel in groups called pods. A single pod can have just two dolphins, but many have up to 40.

There are 33 **species** of dolphins. Most people have seen bottlenose dolphins. They're very smart and can do tricks. They star in shows at zoos and aquariums. Just like other kinds of dolphins, wild bottlenose dolphins live in pods.

Oceans and Rivers

Dolphins live in warm water around the world. Most don't like cold water. Many dolphins, such as bottlenose dolphins, live in Earth's oceans. Four kinds of dolphins live in rivers. Boto dolphins live in rivers in South America.

boto dolphin

Dolphin Friends

Dolphins form close friendships. Males live together in small pods. They join larger pods during the **mating** season. Female dolphins and their young often live together with other females. The members of a pod work together to find food and stay safe.

Superpods!

Sometimes pods come together to form very large pods, or superpods. These pods can have hundreds of dolphins! Some cover several miles of ocean. Superpods sometimes include several different species. They also allow old friends to say hi!

Dolphin Sounds

Dolphins use sounds to **communicate**. Every dolphin makes a special sound so members of the pod can tell each other apart. A baby dolphin, called a calf, quickly learns the sound its mother makes.

Dolphins make sounds that echo, or bounce off objects and come back to them. This tells them how far away something is. It allows them to hunt for fish in cloudy water or when it's dark.

How a Dolphin Echoes

Body Language

Dolphins also communicate by moving and touching each other. They flap their tails or twist in the water. They also rub their heads and bodies against each other. Dolphins can share a lot of thoughts and feelings this way.

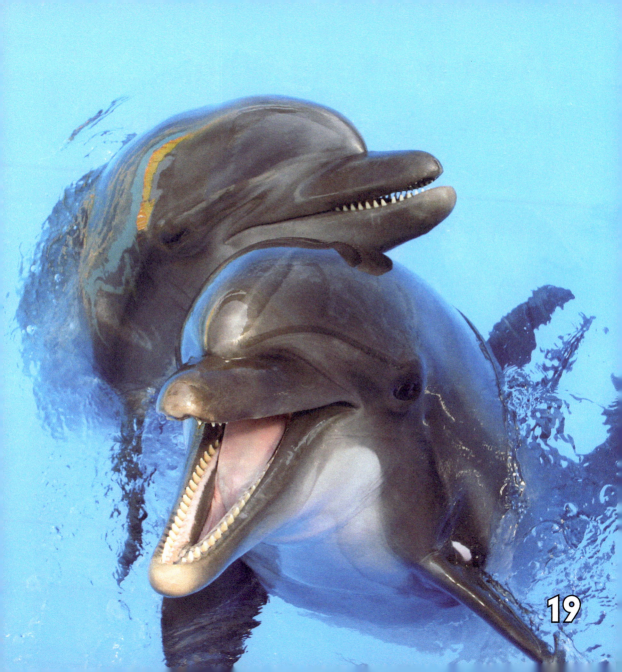

Meet the Killer Whale!

Have you ever heard of a killer whale? These sea mammals aren't whales, they're dolphins! They're the largest dolphins, and they live in oceans all over the world. Killer whales may have a scary name, but most are friendly.

Fun Facts About Killer Whales

Killer whales are also called orcas.

Many killer whales live in very cold waters around Alaska and off the coast of Antarctica.

Killer whales can live up to 80 years in the wild.

An adult killer whale is almost as long as a school bus!

Glossary

communicate: to share feelings or ideas through sounds or motions

mammal: a warm-blooded animal that has a backbone and hair, breathes air, and feeds milk to its young

mating: coming together to make babies

species: a group of plants or animals that are all of the same kind

For More Information

Books

Harris, Caroline. *Whales and Dolphins.* Boston, MA: Kingfisher, 2011.

Stewart, Melissa. *Dolphins.* Washington, DC: National Geographic, 2010.

Websites

Bottlenose Dolphin
animals.nationalgeographic.com/animals/mammals/bottlenose-dolphin/
Learn more about the bottlenose dolphin.

Killer Whale Tales
killerwhaletales.org
This website has tons of information about killer whales and what is being done to keep them safe.

Publisher's note to educators and parents: Our editors have carefully reviewed these websites to ensure that they are suitable for students. Many websites change frequently, however, and we cannot guarantee that a site's future contents will continue to meet our high standards of quality and educational value. Be advised that students should be closely supervised whenever they access the Internet.

Index

Alaska 21
Antarctica 21
aquariums 6
boto dolphins 8
bottlenose dolphins 6, 8
calf 14
cold water 8, 21
communicate 14, 18
echo 16, 17
females 10
friends 10, 12
killer whales 20, 21
males 10
mammals 4, 20
oceans 8, 12, 20

orcas 21
rivers 8
South America 8
species 6, 12
superpods 12
warm water 8
zoos 6